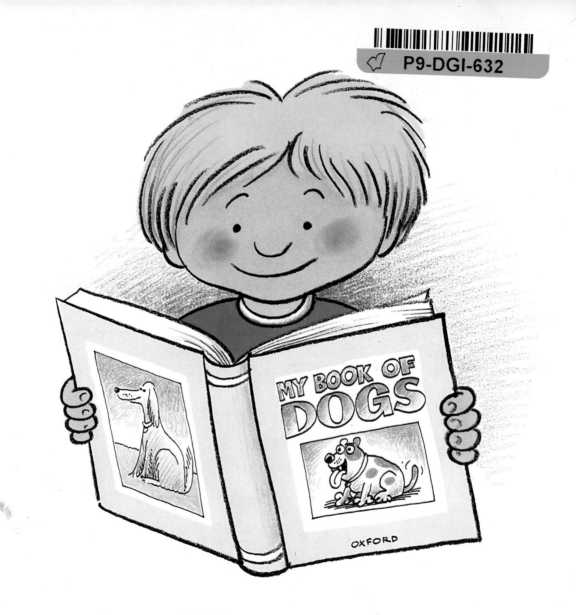

Kipper wanted a dog.

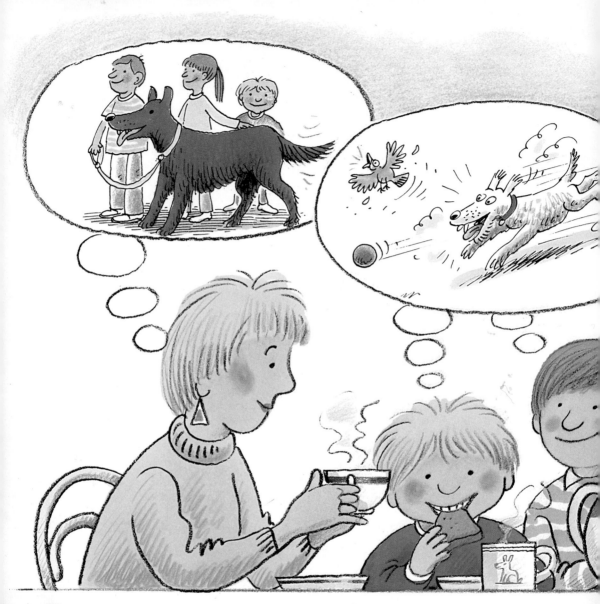

Everyone wanted a dog.

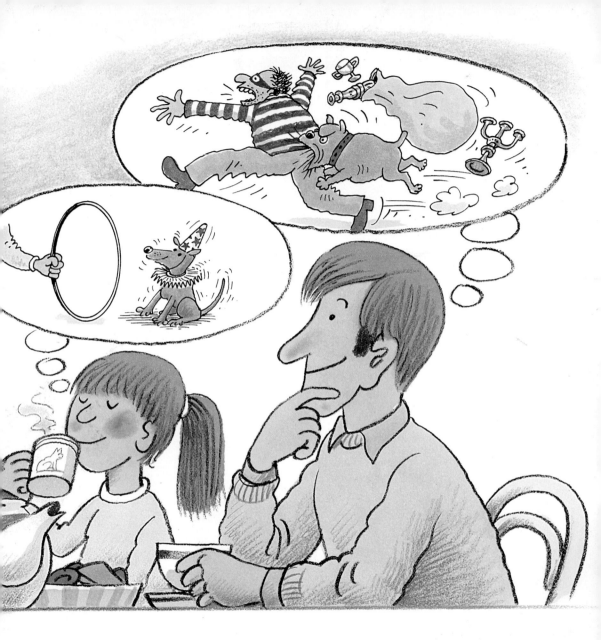

3

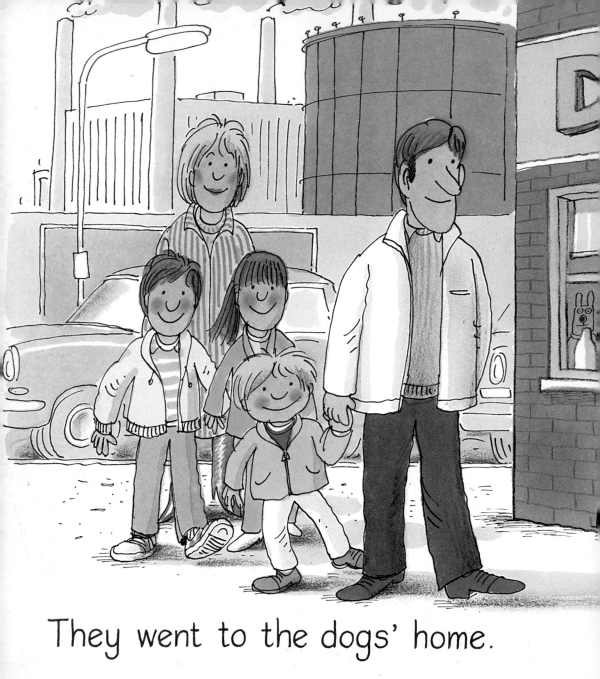

They went to the dogs' home.

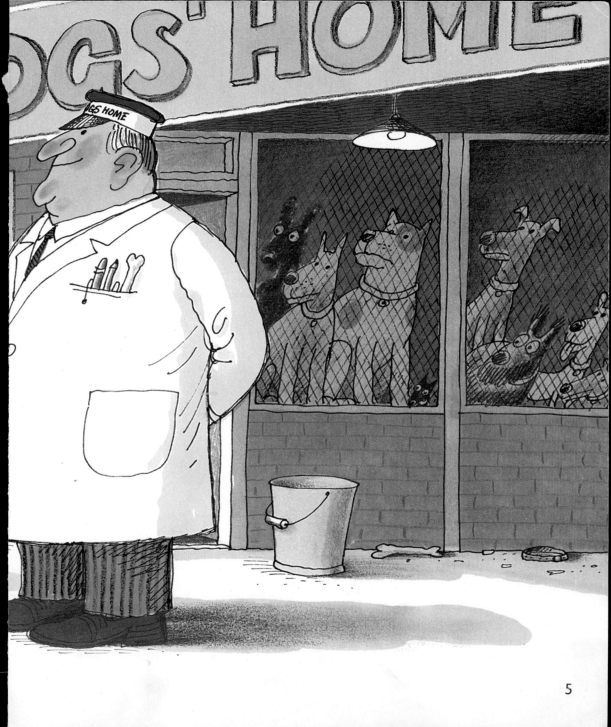

They looked at the dogs.

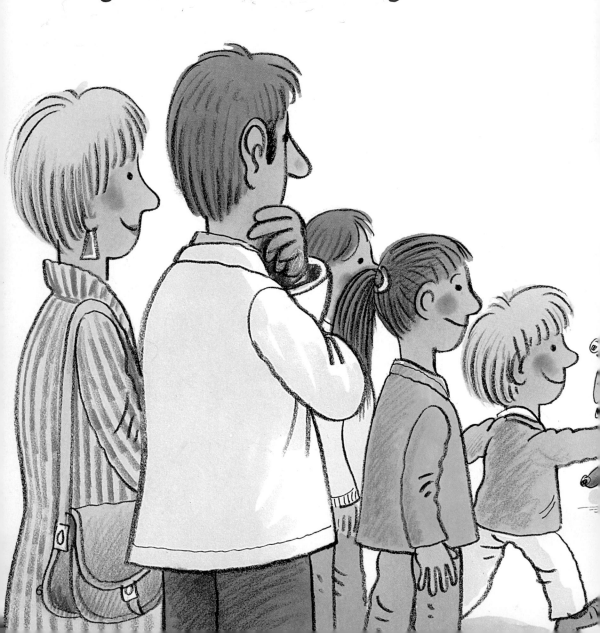

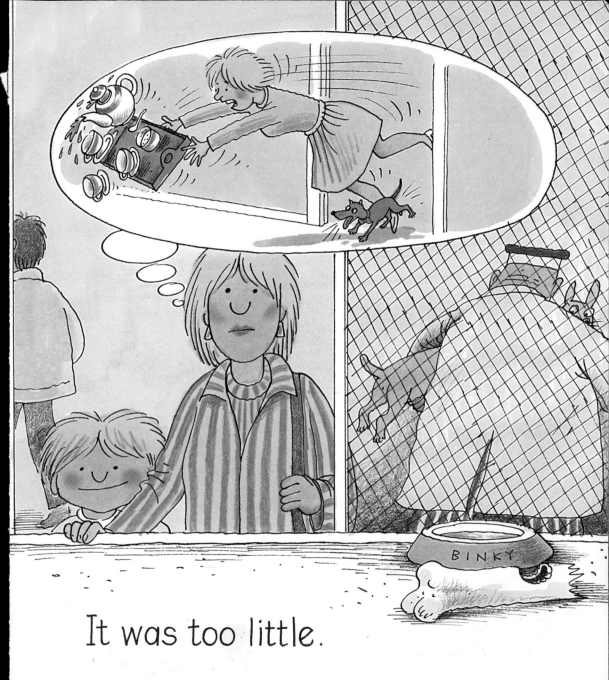

It was too little.

Mum wanted this dog.

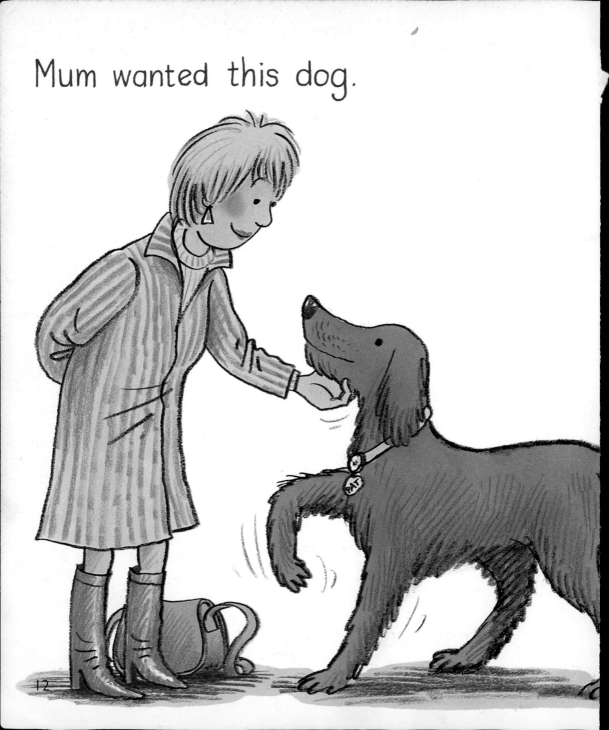

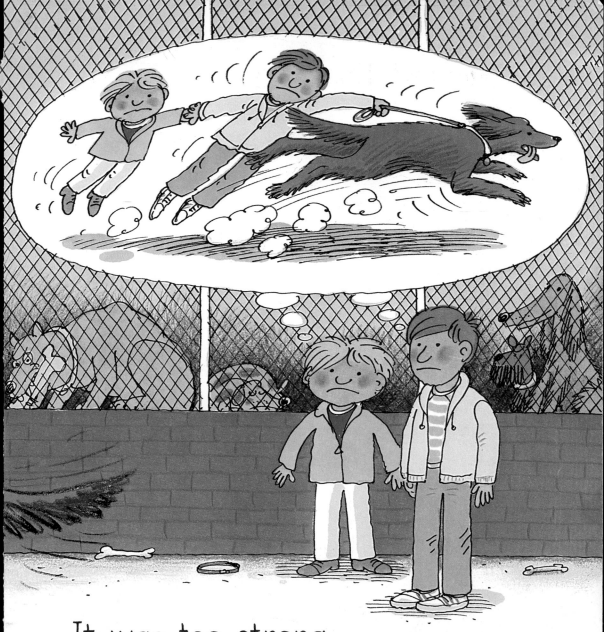

It was too strong.

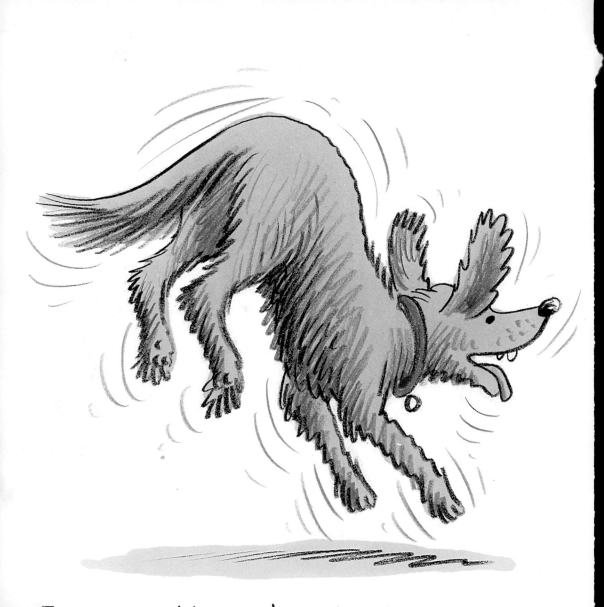

Everyone liked this dog.

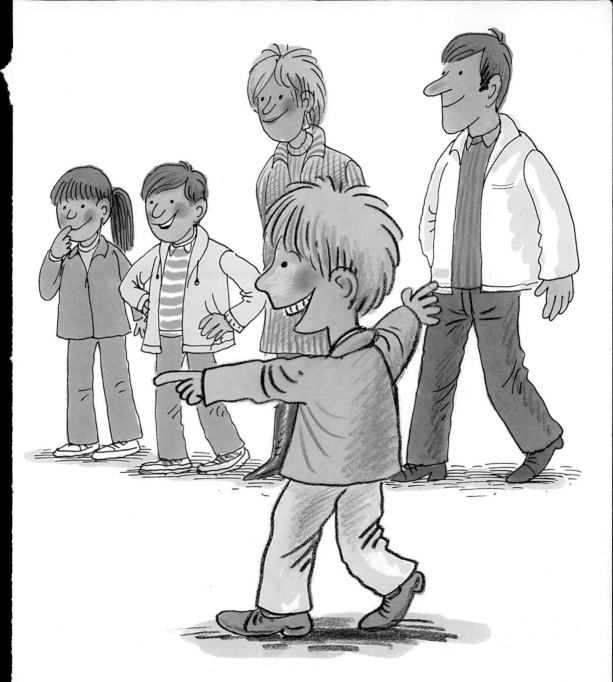

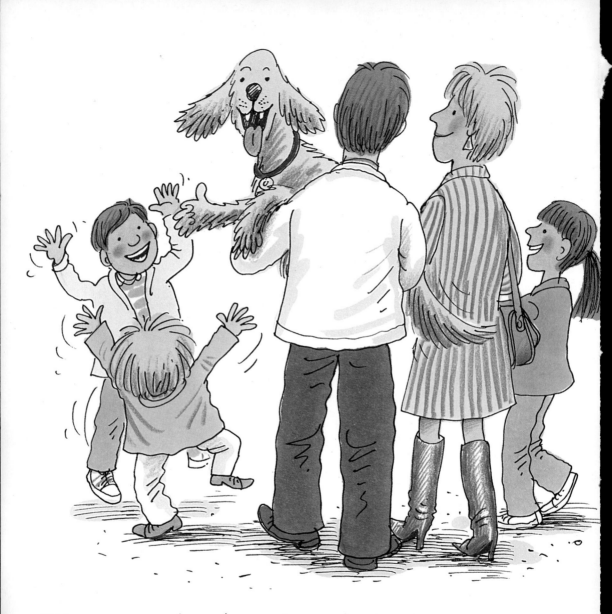

They took the dog home.